D0713037

OXFORD
TOPICS
IN
MUSIC

the synthesizer

john bates

Oxford Topics in Music

Pop Music

Indian Music

The Steel Band

The Piano

The Guitar

Medieval Music

Jamaican Music

Opera

Jazz

The Synthesizer

Acknowledgments

We are grateful to the following for permission to reproduce their material: p. 4 from Marion Melius, 'Music by Electricity', *The World's Work*, June 1906, xii/2; p. 5 (left) Deutsche Staatsbibliothek, East Berlin; p. 6 (left) Bureau de Concerts Maurice Werner, Paris, (right) United Music Publishers/photo Ingi; p. 7 Westdeutscher Rundfunk, Cologne; p. 10 (top) Rom Rhea, Buffalo, New York, (bottom) *Melody Maker*/Elizabeth Walkiden; p. 11 Polydor Records; p. 12 *Melody Maker*/Elizabeth Walkiden; p. 18 Polydor Records; p. 22 Oberheim; p. 23 *Music Technology*; p. 24 (top) *Melody Maker*/photo Janette Beckman, New York, (bottom) Korg UK and Rose-Morris; p. 25 (top left) Roland (UK) Ltd, (bottom left) *Music Technology*, (right) Yamaha-Kemble Music (UK) Ltd; p. 26 (left) Casio Electronics Co Ltd, (right) *Music Technology*; p. 27 *Music Technology*; p. 29 (left) Performing Artservices, New York/photo Narrye Caldwell, (top right) Yamaha-Kemble Music (UK) Ltd, (bottom right) Roland (UK) Ltd; p. 31 WEA Records/photo Paul Rider; p. 32 (left) Virgin Records, (right) Camera Press/photos Charles Steiner; p. 33 Yamaha-Kemble Music (UK) Ltd; p. 34 (left) Fairlight Instruments, (right) *Music Technology*/photo Matthew Vosburgh; p. 35 (left) David Redfern, London, (right) RCA Records; p. 37 *Music Technology*; p. 38 (left) © 1966 Universal Edition (London) Ltd, (right) Crash/Newsfield; Ltd, p. 40 photo Monique Froese, Berlin.

About the series

These short, illustrated information books are designed to explore a range of musical topics of interest to 11–14 year olds. Since reading and fact-gathering should never be a substitute for listening to or playing music a number of suggestions for practical work are included, though in some cases these may be only the starting point for the musical work that could be related to a particular topic. The books can be used in a variety of ways: for example, three together might form the core for class, group or individual work. For older children, the books would be a useful source of reference for examination projects.

© John Bates 1988

First published 1988

ISBN 0 19 321337 0

Photoset by Rowland Phototypesetting Ltd
Bury St Edmunds, Suffolk
Printed in Hong Kong

The Synthesizer

John Bates

Oxford University Press
Music Department,
Walton Street, Oxford OX2 6DP

Contents

Introduction

It is almost impossible to spend a day without hearing music and sound created by a synthesizer. Much of the music for television and radio uses music produced by electronic means. Pop music features synthesizers on almost every record; films, musicals, and plays all use synthesizers. But what exactly is a synthesizer?

To synthesize means to combine basic elements together. If we think for a moment of a paint box which has only black, red, yellow, blue and white it is possible to create any colour by mixing these in varying degrees. What a synthesizer does is to create the basic elements of sound electronically and allow you to mix them together.

The synthesizer is the most important and the most influential instrument invented since the piano. It is a product of this century and will continue to develop with us as we grow older. At present there is no end in sight to its capabilities both as a musical instrument and as a creator of sounds. Before we find out how it works we are going to have a look at the instruments and composers that have encouraged the development of the synthesizer.

Throughout the book there will be projects that can be carried out on either a synthesizer or a micro-computer. How much can be achieved on the micro-computer depends on the model you are using and the program that is running it. There are many programs available which turn micro-computers into some form of sound synthesizer. If you are thinking of buying such a program it is well worth reading through some of the many computer magazines available to make sure that the program will do what you require. At the back of this book is a list of music programs that are worth looking at as a further guide. If you do use a micro-computer please consult the manual for it so that you can be sure of what you are doing. A word of caution here—many of the micro-computers generate envelopes that are far more complex than those shown in this book. They are able to repeat sounds quickly and alter the actual pitch of the note.

1 The history of the synthesizer

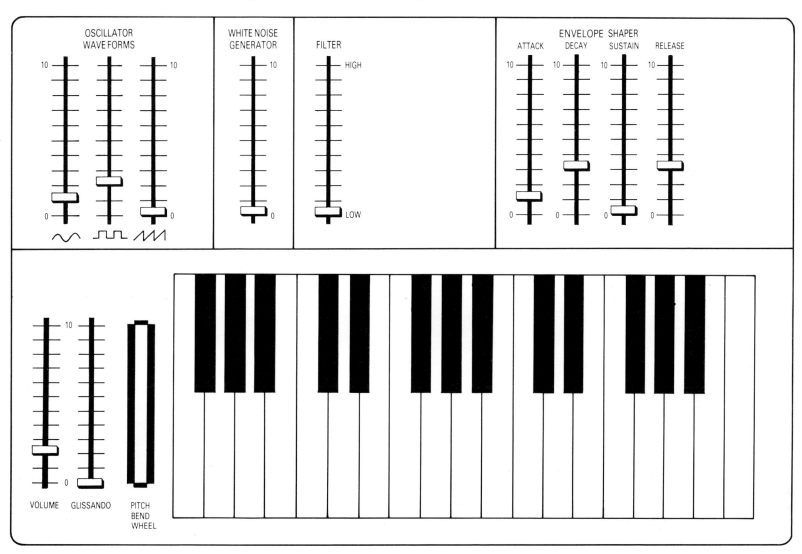

A modern synthesizer looks something like this.

Like many inventions—hi-fi systems, television, videos, and computers—the development of the synthesizer has depended on components becoming cheaper and smaller. We have therefore three distinct ages: valves, transistors, and the micro-chip. In this section we will talk about valves and transistors. The age of the micro-chip will be discussed in a later section.

▼ Dynamophone

The age of the valve

◀ A valve

Valves look a little bit like light bulbs. They were developed between 1902 and 1917. They were first used in the earliest radios but came to be used for creating sounds electronically as well as transmitting and receiving sound.

Cahill's dynamophone

Synthesizers are thought of as a modern invention, rather like the micro-computer. It may come as a surprise to find that the first instrument to create sound by using electricity was demonstrated as long ago as 1906 by an American scientist and inventor Thaddeus Cahill (1867–1934). He called it a 'dynamophone' or a 'telharmonium'. By today's standards it would sound rather strange and not very good but unfortunately there are no existing recordings of the instrument. The instrument weighed over 200 tons and was made partly from telephone exchange components. It was eventually dumped into the sea off New York.

Ferruccio Busoni (1866–1924), a famous composer and pianist, wrote in 1907 that music could become far greater through instruments like this 'a vista of fair hopes and dream-like fancies'—a dream come true.

In the fifty or so years following this, radio and television developed. They spread into many countries and to improve them more electronic parts were invented.

Using the latest technology available many early synthesizers were invented. They had names like spherophone, partiturophone, trautonium, mellertion,

◀ Busoni

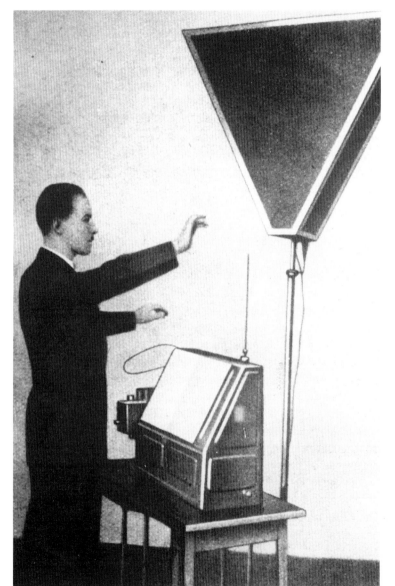

emicon and hellertion. Most of these are forgotten today but two that are still remembered are the 'theremin' and the 'ondes martenot', both named after their inventors.

The theremin and the ondes martenot

The theremin was first demonstrated in Petrograd (now known as Leningrad), USSR in August 1920 and was originally called the 'aetherophone'. Its sound was created by the player moving his hands away from or closer to a central aeriel. By 1924 a special work had been written for the instrument, *Symphonic Mystery for theremin and orchestra* by a composer called Pashchenko. This was probably the first work ever written for an electronic instrument. In 1927 the inventor Leon Theremin took the instrument to America and patented it. It was produced in several different versions and was still being produced in the 1950s. It was used as late as 1966 by the American pop group The Beach Boys in their hit 'Good Vibrations'.

▲ Theremin

It is almost certain that the Frenchman, Maurice Martenot, saw an early demonstration of the theremin and this led him to develop the ondes martenot (pronounced ond mar–ten-oh)—the name means Martenot's Waves.

The importance of these instruments was first seen by the serious composers and musicians. The pop musicians of the time did not take them seriously, although three theremins were briefly used for dance music in New York in 1931. Both instruments have been much used in film music, the first being the theremin in the music for *King Kong* in 1933 by Max Steiner.

Varèse

Edgard Varèse (1883–1965) was a composer who grew up in the age when synthesizers were few and far between. However he was a composer who very soon realized the potential of using sound for its own sake. Some of his pieces do not use tunes but effects of sound that form patterns. The work for percussion—*Ionisation* (1917) is a good example of this. He very quickly saw the potential of the early synthesizers '. . . I dream of instruments obedient to my thought and . . . of a whole new world of unsuspected sounds . . .'

Ecuatorial (1934) was written using two theremins which he later changed to ondes martenots. Some of his later works do not use synthesizers as such but use pre-recorded tapes of organized electronic sound, for example *Deserts* (1954).

Messiaen

The French composer Olivier Messiaen (b. 1908) uses an ondes martenot as part of the orchestra in his work *Turangalîla-symphonie* which was written in 1948. Listen to the last movement and see if you can pick out the highpitched sliding notes of the ondes martenot.

▲ Ondes martenot played by Jeanne Loriod.

Olivier Messiaen ▶

Electronic music studios

After the second world war (1939–45) the development of electronics began to speed up. Several electronic music studios were founded in the early 1950s in Europe, America and Japan (see map on page 8). The instruments which composers now used had become very big and were difficult to use in a concert hall, though this did not present a problem because the tape recorder had been recently greatly improved. Composers could record on to tape the sounds

and music they created and did not have to perform live. One of the most prominent composers of the 1950s to do this was the German composer Karlheinz Stockhausen.

Stockhausen

Karlheinz Stockhausen (b. 1928) has written many works using electronically created sound. He does not use a complete synthesizer as we know it but the separate modules (see chapter 2) that form a synthesizer. His music is often very carefully planned using many calculations to ensure that the

Stockhausen in an early electronic music studio.

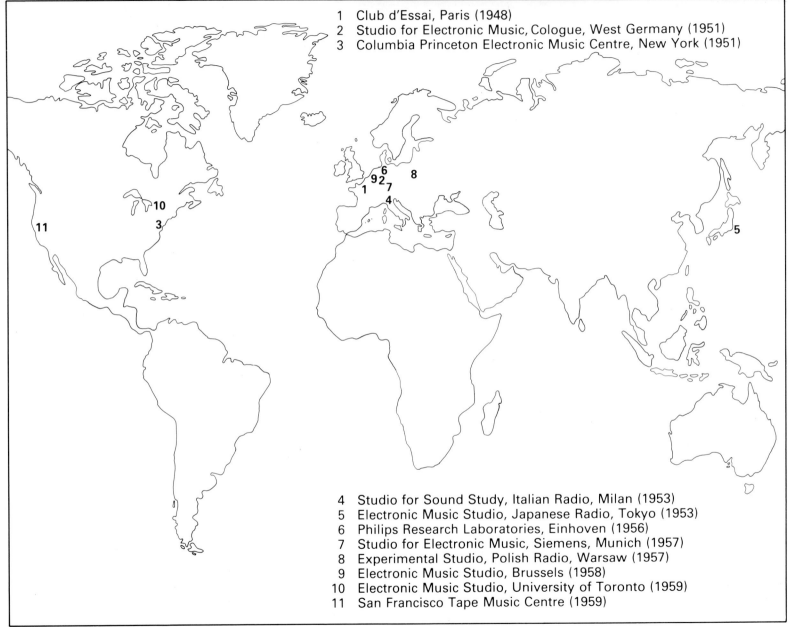

1 Club d'Essai, Paris (1948)
2 Studio for Electronic Music, Cologue, West Germany (1951)
3 Columbia Princeton Electronic Music Centre, New York (1951)

4 Studio for Sound Study, Italian Radio, Milan (1953)
5 Electronic Music Studio, Japanese Radio, Tokyo (1953)
6 Philips Research Laboratories, Einhoven (1956)
7 Studio for Electronic Music, Siemens, Munich (1957)
8 Experimental Studio, Polish Radio, Warsaw (1957)
9 Electronic Music Studio, Brussels (1958)
10 Electronic Music Studio, University of Toronto (1959)
11 San Francisco Tape Music Centre (1959)

▲ Map showing electronic music studios in the 1950s. Electronic music studios did not emerge in Great Britain until the mid–1960s.

sounds are linked and related mathematically. The scores for his music are often very detailed and look like graphs (see Music notation page 38). For much of the 1950s he worked in the electronic music studios in Cologne. Much of his music is a blend of electronic and orchestral instruments in unusual ways. Some of his works have used radios as part of their sound! *Studie* (1954) is one of the first purely electronic pieces of music. The discography has a list of some more pieces you may like to listen to.

In America in 1952 the RCA company built a very large electronic instrument that used a computer to help it work. This was the first instrument to be called a synthesizer. Unfortunately, the music and sounds produced in this era were not easily understood by many people who were more used to the conventional orchestral instruments and concerts.

Questions

1 When was the first instrument that made sound by electricity invented?
2 What were the two best known early electronic instruments called? Who invented them?
3 Which composer pioneered electronic music in the 1950s?

Projects

1 Listen to part of *Ecuatorial* by Varèse and also listen to 'Good Vibrations' by the Beach Boys. Both these pieces of music use a theremin. Which do you think uses the theremin best? Why?
2 Listen to *Ionisation* by Varèse. Are there any tunes that you can remember? Do you think that the piece would be better if there were more tunes?
3 Find out all you can about Stockhausen or Varèse.

The age of the transistor

The bulky and somewhat unreliable valve was replaced in about 1963 by the much smaller and reliable transistor. This was also much cheaper to make.

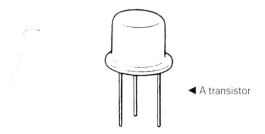

◀ A transistor

Dr Robert Moog

Soon after this an American, Dr Robert Moog (b. 1934), developed the first synthesizer that anybody could buy. Although still quite large it was nevertheless portable. Not only did it use electricity to *create* sound but it also used electricity to *control* the sound. This is called voltage control. The first Moog synthesizer resembled several large boxes, (modules), that could be connected to each other by leads. Each box performed a particular electronic function and different sounds were created by altering the controls on the electronic boxes or by changing the way in which each box connected to another, re-ordering them. This is called modular synthesis and is still used in some systems today. The leads joining the parts were called patch cords. This has led to the term 'patch' meaning the way the controls are set on a synthesizer to create a particular sound.

Dr Robert Moog has been called the father of the modern synthesizer. A record made by Walter Carlos in 1968 called

▲ Robert A. Moog with three synthesizers designed by him: a Moog Modular System Series 900 *c*.1964 (*rear*), the Minimoog Model D *c*.1970 (*foreground right*), and the Moog Sonic Six, *c*.1970.

▼ Keith Emerson of Emerson Lake and Palmer at a Moog synthesizer.

Switched on Bach consisted of the music of J. S. Bach played entirely on Moog synthesizers. It was a very popular record and introduced the synthesizer to a great many people. The name Moog became almost another word for synthesizer. Now the instrument was portable and quite versatile, it came within the reach of pop groups.

A very small version called a Mini-Moog was produced in 1970 and this quickly became one of the most popular synthesizers. It did not use patch cords but used switches to connect the various sound-creating elements. It had a built-in keyboard and was contained in one small unit, thus being the first truly portable synthesizer. It was this instrument that introduced the idea and the sound of the synthesizers to everybody. Although monophonic it had a wide range of sounds and effects. It was very quickly taken up by many rock bands of the early 1970s and became a feature on many records.

Its wide variety of sounds appealed to pop musicians. Some groups like ELP and Roxy Music in the early 1970s used this instrument as a distinctive part of their sound.

Emerson Lake and Palmer

They were one of the first groups to use Moog synthesizers on record and on stage. The classically trained keyboard player Keith Emerson co-operated with Robert Moog in perfecting the design of the Mini-Moog which you can hear being played on 'Lucky Man' from their first LP *Emerson Lake and Palmer*.

Roxy Music

The original synthesizer player with this group was Brian Eno. He created many unusual effects and sounds which were a feature of their early records. He always described himself as a non-musician—an artist working with sound. You can hear the Mini-Moog on their record 'Virginia Plain' (1972). Soon

▲ Roxy Music, with Brian Eno seated left, 1973.

after this other manufacturers started to produce similar instruments. They were easy to play, easy to carry about, and capable of many sounds—the synthesizer explosion had begun.

Questions

1 Who was the first person to make a synthesizer that anybody could buy?
2 What does the word patch mean when referring to synthesizers?
3 What record made the synthesizer very popular and well known to many people?

Projects

1 Carry out a survey.
i Find out how many people:
  a have a synthesizer.
  b have a home computer. If so, do they use it to create sounds or music?
  c have an organ.
  d have a small keyboard.
  e have a piano.
  f have an instrument not mentioned above.
ii a Do they play these instruments: once a day, once a week, once a month, never?
  b If some people do not have any instruments at all, ask them what instrument they would like to play.
iii Ask each person what instrument they would like to play if they had a choice.
iv From your results find out which instrument most people would like to play. Is this the same as the instruments which they have at home? How popular are synthesizers and electronic instruments?

11

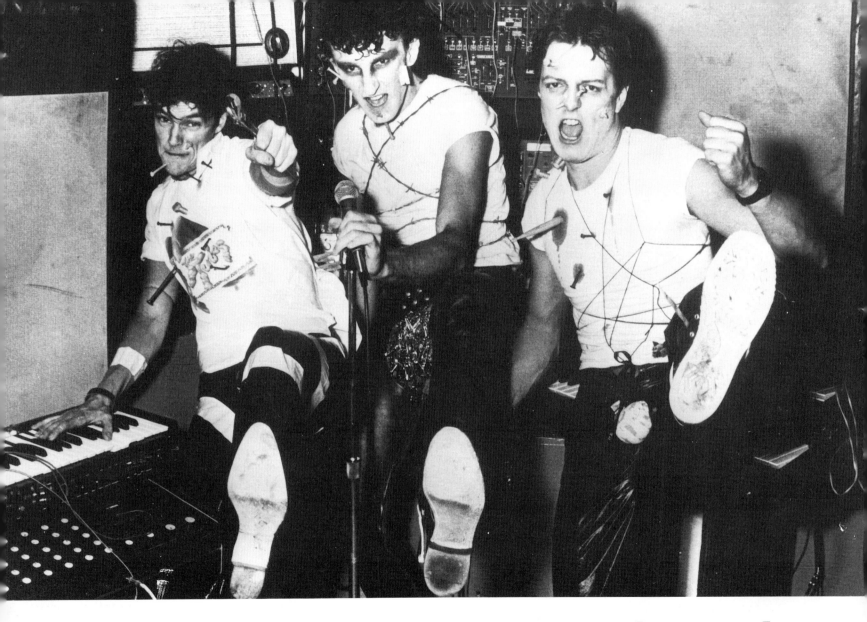

2 How a synthesizer works and sounds

How sound sounds

Ours is a world full of sound. If you stop reading this for a few seconds and listen to all that you can hear you will find that there are sounds going on all the time: birds singing, cars moving, water dripping, people talking in the room next door, perhaps even music playing. All these sounds are created by vibrations in the air.

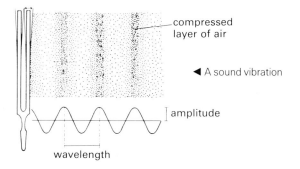

compressed layer of air

◄ A sound vibration

amplitude

wavelength

A synthesizer has no moving strings or vibrating parts like other instruments. It relies on electricity to create its sound. By making electrical signals vibrate (oscillate) in different ways it is possible to create sound. The heart of a synthesizer is the electronic part that does this, called an **oscillator**. Many of the early electronic instruments were basically oscillators.

Painting sounds

Creating a sound on a synthesizer is rather like painting a picture. In order to paint a picture, first the colours that are going to be used are mixed. Then some of the colours are thinned down with water so that they are not so bright. Finally the colours are put on to paper by the artist who has decided on the shape of the picture to be painted.

◄ The Tubes (*left to right*: Mike Cotten, Fee Waybill, Prairie Prince; (see page 18)).

If we put down these steps in order they would look something like this:

1 **Mix** the colours together.
2 **Thin** some of the colours down.
3 Paint the various colours on to paper in definite **shapes** to create a picture.

Some modern synthesizers use more complex variations developed from this idea, see DX synthesizers on page 29.

Mixing the basic sounds

We can think of sound rather like a paintbox. In a paintbox there are primary colours that we can mix to make colours. A synthesizer has three basic primary sounds that we can mix together to produce different colours of sound. These primary sounds are called **waves**. If we could look at sound with the aid of a special piece of equipment called an oscilloscope we would see that the primary waves look like this:

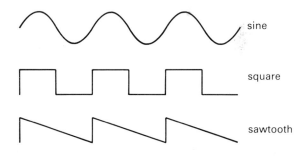

sine

square

sawtooth

In a synthesizer these can be mixed together to produce different sounds. In a paintbox there are many colours we can mix. In a synthesizer there are many sounds we can mix. In the language of the synthesizer mixing sounds together is called **modulating**. In the diagram of a basic synthesizer you can see the waveform section to the left (page 3).

Thinning the sound

Although we have created a sound we may find that this sound is too harsh or too dull. In the paintbox, water can be used to tone down the colour. In a synthesizer we use a **filter**. This is somewhat similar in effect to the tone controls on a hi-fi that you may have in your school or home. On a hi-fi system there are usually controls that make either the high sounds (treble) or the low sounds (bass) louder. A synthesizer uses a filter to remove the sounds that are not wanted. It works rather like a pair of sunglasses. Sunglasses prevent harsh light from coming into your eyes. They do this by filtering out the bright light. In a synthesizer the filter can be adjusted to stop either bright or dull sounds passing through.

If we could see the sound, this is how a filter set to allow high sounds to pass through would appear.

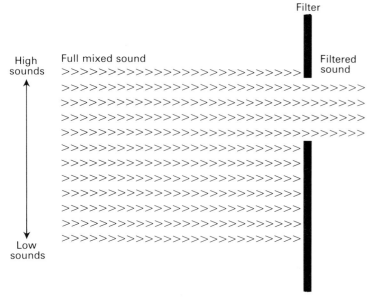

▲ The filter has only allowed a small amount of the full sound through. The filter section appears in the middle of the synthesizer diagram (page 3).

14

Shaping sound

Now we have made the basic sound it has to be formed into a shape. All sounds, whether from a musical instrument or not, have a certain shape. Some sounds or noises are short and sharp. If you clap your hands together the sound is very short and usually quite loud. Other sounds are longer and not so sharp. The sound of a bell will last after it has been struck.

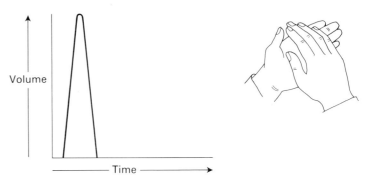

▲ The sound shape of the handclap is straight up and almost straight down again. This is because the sound is loud immediately and finishes as quickly as it starts.

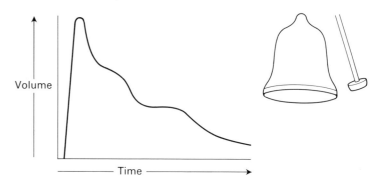

▲ The sound shape of the bell is much longer. After the hammer has hit the bell the sound carries on, gradually getting quieter and quieter.

The proper name of each soundshape is an **envelope**.

Synthesizers have an **envelope shaper** or **envelope generator** which usually has four sliding controls. These are:

Attack—controls how quickly the sound increases in volume after the key is pressed

Decay—controls how soon the sound will start to fade away

Sustain—controls how long the sound will stay if the key is held down

Release—controls how long the sound takes to die away after the key is released

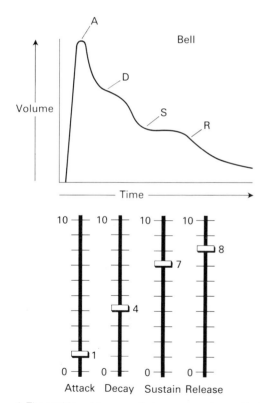

▲ The position of these controls corresponds roughly to the shape of the sound we have drawn but upside down. So in order to create the envelope of a bell we would need to set our envelope controls something like this.

The envelope shaper is on the right hand side of the synthesizer diagram (page 3).

Some modern synthesizers have no sliding controls at all. They use figures for each part of the sound which have to be put into its memory rather like a calculator or computer. This makes it rather difficult to see the shape of the sound you are creating. When we are using micro-computers to make sounds you will see that we can only tell the computer in terms of figures (e.g. 1 is a very fast attack, 10 is very slow).

The way in which sounds are created on a synthesizer are therefore:

MIX $\longrightarrow$ FILTER $\longrightarrow$ SHAPE $\longrightarrow$ SOUND

which correspond to the ways in which the artist paints a picture.

It is possible to draw the shapes of these sounds on paper.

Questions

1 What device does a synthesizer use to create its sound?
2 What is a wave?
3 What does modulating mean?
4 What does a filter do to the sound?
5 What is the proper name for the shape of a sound?

Projects

1 Try this experiment to show how vibrations create sound. Place a metal ruler or comb on the edge of a table or desk so that at least half is overhanging the edge. Press down firmly to hold the ruler or comb to the desk and flick the end that is overhanging. What happens if the length overhanging is shortened or lengthened?
2 Make a list of several instruments that you are easily able to hear played. Get some friends or people who can play

to play one note on each instrument. Try to draw a sound envelope for each instrument. (It might help if you could use a cassette recorder to tape each one.)

Compare and see which envelope was the shortest or the longest. Which had the fastest attack?

You could try to guess the instruments by looking at the envelope. The following list may be useful:

recorder   cymbal
guitar   wood block
violin   someone whistling one note
triangle

3   Using a micro-computer or synthesizer listen to the different waveforms it can create. You could test your memory by having a friend play them and you could guess which one is being played.

4   Using a micro-computer or synthesizer listen to what happens when a waveform is filtered. Which waveform is affected the most? Be sure to write down what you find out as you can use this to refer to the next time you use the instrument.

High or low; loud or quiet

When we listen to sounds there are things about them that we often take for granted. Our ears sometimes overlook the fact that some sounds are high, some are low, some are louder than others.

The sound of a big lorry or the double-bass in an orchestra

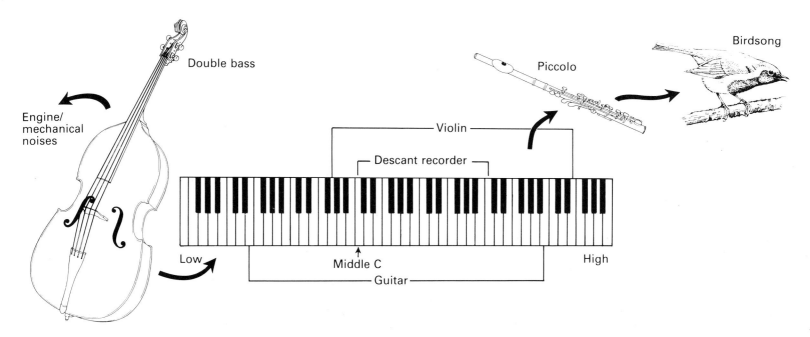

Double bass

Engine/ mechanical noises

Piccolo

Birdsong

Violin

Descant recorder

Low

Middle C

High

Guitar

are examples of low sounds. They sound deep and low down. The sound of a bird singing or the piccolo in the orchestra are high sounds. Before we complete our sound picture we have to instruct the synthesizer to play either a high, middle, or low sound. Some sounds which are pleasant when played high are quite menacing when played low.

Nearly all synthesizers are played with a keyboard which looks like that of a small piano or organ. If you have ever sat down at these instruments and played them you will know that the keys to your left produce the low sounds and the keys to your right produce the high sounds. Many synthesizers have quite small keyboards. To help them play high and low notes they have a special switch which can make the whole keyboard play either the lowest or highest range of notes. In this way although they have small keyboards, they can play a wide range of sounds. The word that describes the height or depth of a note is **pitch**.

Pitch is often described on a synthesizer in terms of feet! This is because on church organs the pipes are of certain lengths to sound either higher or lower. The term was passed

on to cinema organs and then to home organs. Most synthesizers use this system of describing the height or depth of sounds although some now use note names and octave number: e.g. middle C = C3.

Sounds in everyday life are loud or quiet and the synthesizer is equipped with a volume control to make the sound as loud or quiet as you want it. Some sounds will need more volume than others. This is because they are less noticeable to our ears. They seem to be softer although they are in fact using the same amount of basic waves and filtering as louder, more shrill sounds.

White noise

When you are trying to find a programme on your radio and you are between stations you may hear a sort of hissing sound. This is called **white noise**. This sound is very useful to someone creating sounds on a synthesizer. Most synthesizers have a **white noise generator** that creates this sound. On its own it is not much use but when it is altered by filters and envelopes it can be made to sound like the sea or wind. Sometimes it is mixed with other sounds to create different effects. It is often used in films like *Star Wars* or *The Empire Strikes Back* to create 'spacey' effects.

The white noise generator is just to the left of the filter in the diagram (page 3).

Glissando

This is the effect of sliding between notes. Most synthesizers have a control for this. The more you increase the control, the slower the note will slide.

Pitch bend

The wheel on the left of the diagram (page 3) will raise or lower the pitch of a note being played. It will only lift it up a small amount. Usually it is done very quickly to give a 'bending' effect to the note, similar to that of plucking a guitar or violin string while turning the tuning peg.

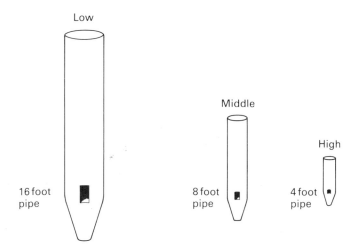

▲ A four foot pitch is an octave higher than an eight foot. A sixteen foot pitch is an octave lower.

▲ Vangelis

Vangelis

The Greek-born composer Vangelis uses synthesizers combined with other instruments to create very effective music and sounds. His best known work is the music from the film *Chariots of Fire* (1980). Try to listen to this and decide when he is using synthesizers and when he is using acoustic instruments. He is a good example of a composer who uses sound colours.

The Tubes

Although they are well known in America for their theatrical shows, The Tubes' first LP used both synthesizers and orchestra mixed together. Mike Cotten who plays synthesizers has never played any other instrument.

Imitating other instruments

Let us suppose that you want your synthesizer to sound like a clarinet. The soundwave that is closest to a clarinet is a square wave. On its own without any filtering or shaping the sound is not very good. It is too harsh and abrupt. If you have a clarinet or know someone who can play a clarinet then listen to the sound of it. The note starts gently and does not get loud immediately. It then reaches its loudest point and remains quite loud as long as the player has enough breath. The sound cuts off as soon as the note has ended. This can be translated onto the envelope shaper as follows:

note starts gently = slowish attack
note remains loud = long sustain/no decay
note cuts off after = no release

The setting of sound filters can be adjusted until it sounds like a clarinet.

Generally, the waveforms on synthesizers sound like this:

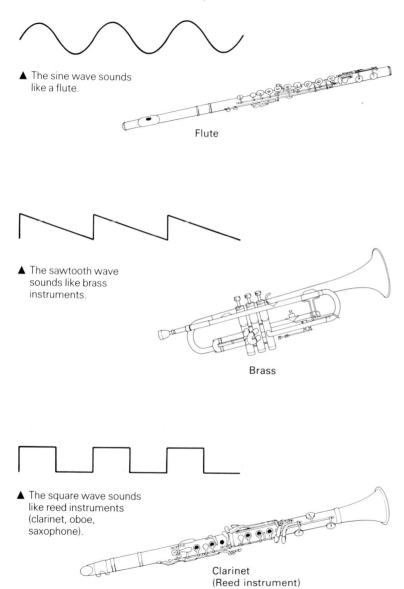

▲ The sine wave sounds like a flute.

Flute

▲ The sawtooth wave sounds like brass instruments.

Brass

▲ The square wave sounds like reed instruments (clarinet, oboe, saxophone).

Clarinet
(Reed instrument)

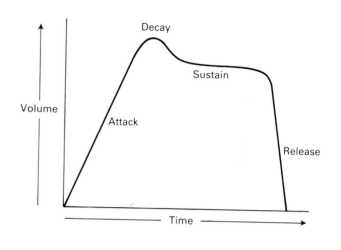

Decay

Volume

Attack

Sustain

Release

Time

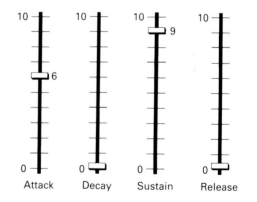

| 10 | 10 | 10 | 10 |
| Attack | Decay | Sustain | Release |

6 Attack, 9 Sustain

▲ Try this using a square wave set at 8' pitch C3.

Other ways of altering the sound

Having created the sound with the envelope that you want, there are several ways to alter the sound. Many instruments have a sound that has **vibrato** within it. Vibrato is when the pitch of the note moves very slightly up and down. A good example of this is the violin. Ask someone who can play the violin reasonably well to show you. You will see that the finger holding the string on the neck of the violin wobbles to and fro. As it does the pitch of the note varies slightly. It has the effect of making the note more interesting and musically effective to listen to. It is most effective on long sustained notes.

Other instruments which use vibrato are:

'cello	flute
viola	guitar, both electric and acoustic
clarinet	oboe
saxophone	trumpet

A good example of guitar vibrato can be heard on the Beatles track 'While my guitar gently weeps' from the *White Album*.

The vibrato effect is created on a synthesizer by a **low frequency oscillator**, which is a device that generates waveforms that are so slow that we cannot hear them. Instead of hearing this as a sound it is used to alter the pitch of the note by connecting it to the main oscillator. By adjusting the level we can create a note that has vibrato.

If the low frequency oscillator is connected to the filter then it makes the sound appear to 'sweep' across. This is often done in connection with white noise to imitate the sound of the sea or the wind. Different waveforms give slightly different vibrato effects. The most commonly used is the sine wave. This gives an even rise and fall pitch. A square wave makes the pitch step up and down.

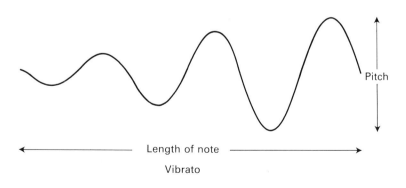

Length of note

Pitch

Vibrato

▲ Vibrato on a violin, and the sound wave it causes

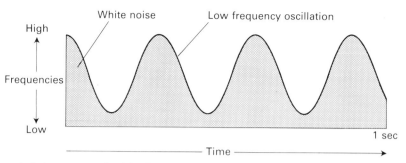

High

Frequencies

Low

White noise   Low frequency oscillation

1 sec

Time

▲ A sine wave used to 'chop' white noise to create wind and sea effects.

Questions

1 What is pitch? What measurement does a synthesizer use for pitch? Why?
2 What is glissando?
3 What waveform sounds like a flute?
4 What waveform sounds like a trumpet?
5 What is vibrato? How can we create it on a synthesizer?

Projects

1 Draw a diagram of a piano keyboard, putting an arrow against middle C. Using brackets mark the range of as many instruments as possible. Use reference books to help you find out the range of the instruments.
2 Make a list of some of the instruments you might find in an orchestra. Decide whether they are brass, reed, string, or something else. Make a note on your list which category each instrument belongs to. Find out which instruments are high pitched, low pitched, or somewhere in the middle.

   In the last column decide which waveform would be best suited for the instrument.

3 Create a sound on the micro-computer or synthesizer using a waveform and filter. See what happens to the sound you have created when it is put through the envelope (ADSR) on your micro-computer or synthesizer. Using the same sound try:
   a A very fast attack and decay.
   b A very fast attack, long sustain.
   c A long slow attack, short sustain, slow decay.
   Does the amount of attack given to a sound alter the effect of the decay?
   Write down which settings create the best or worst sounds.

3 The age of the micro-chip

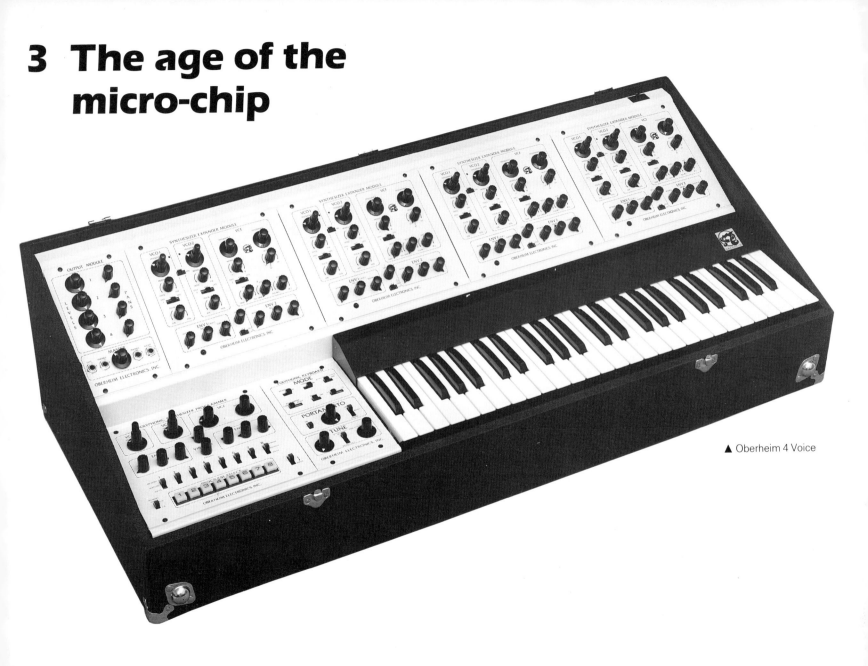

▲ Oberheim 4 Voice

Before about 1974 most synthesizers had been monophonic. That is to say they could only play one note at a time, just as a recorder, trumpet, or clarinet can. With the development of the integrated circuit, or micro-chip as it came to be known, polyphonic instruments started to appear. Polyphonic means that it can play three or more notes at once. Most polyphonic synthesizers can play six, eight, or sixteen notes at the same time. A piano is capable of sounding every note at the same time, i.e. it is a totally polyphonic instrument. From 1974 onwards more and more synthesizers were produced of many different makes and types.

The first polyphonic synthesizer was made by the American company Oberheim in 1974. It was called the Oberheim 4 Voice and was in effect four Mini-Moogs in one. You could play four notes at a time.

A disadvantage of many of the early synthesizers was the time it took to create a particular sound. If a musician was working in a recording studio this was not too annoying as once the sound had been recorded it had been preserved on

▼ Prophet–5 (*centre*) and Minimoog (*right*) belonging to Tangerine Dream.

tape. If the musician was playing on stage it meant that only a few simple sounds could be used. To overcome this synthesizers were made with memories for sounds. When a musician created a sound the synthesizer was capable of memorizing it.

Prophet–5

The first completely programable polyphonic synthesizer was the Prophet–5, launched in 1977. It was built by the American company Sequential Circuits and quickly became one of the most popular synthesizers. It used the same micro-chip as the Sinclair ZX81 computer to memorize the different sounds created by the player. It can store up to 120 sounds created by the performer.

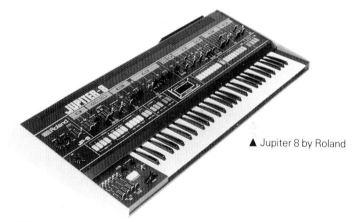

▲ Jupiter 8 by Roland

Roland Jupiter 8

The Jupiter 8 has a large memory for storing sounds. This meant that a performer on stage could simply press a number and the sound he had created and stored would appear. This was a great help, the performer did not have to spend time actually creating the sound on stage. It could also play one sound with the lower half of the keyboard and another with the upper half. This is called a 'split keyboard'.

Special synthesizers

There are some synthesizers that are made for certain functions only. Some for example sound like drums. Others will use the sound of the human voice and translate it into synthesized sounds. A synthesizer that does this is called a **vocoder**. A vocoder takes the sound of the voice through the microphone and into the synthesizer. It is then altered inside the synthesizer by filters and envelopes. Some vocoders will work in conjunction with the keyboard so that the voice will sound only at the pitch of the notes played. A good example of this is the song 'Mr Blue Sky' by the Electric Light Orchestra.

Drum machines and units

One definition of a drum synthesizer is a machine that has different drum sounds on it. The user can then play different rhythm patterns using combinations of these drums. This could be used to form the basis of a song.

Most home organs have a drum unit with them. However the drum kit will usually only play pre-set patterns put into it by the manufacturer.

◀ Laurie Anderson

▼ Vocoder by Korg

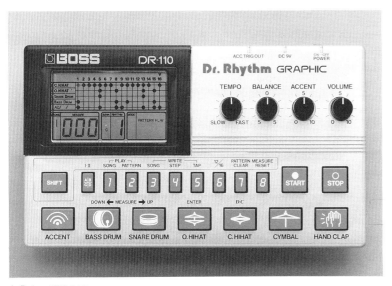

▲ Roland DR 110

▼ The Synsonics drum machine is a fully programable drum machine. It also has four touch-sensitive pads which can be played either with the fingers or drum sticks.

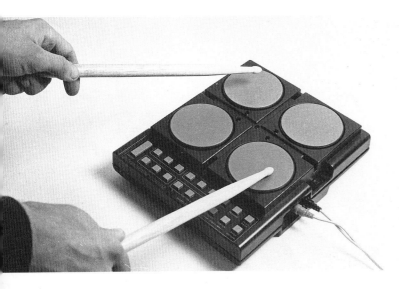

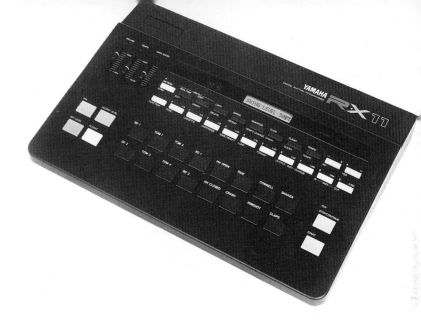

▲ The RX11 uses the sound of real drums stored on micro-chip. It can store many rhythm patterns and can be connected to other synthesizers, acting as a clock for other sequenced patterns.

Questions

1 What is a monophonic synthesizer?
2 What is the advantage of a programable synthesizer?
3 What is a vocoder?

Projects

1 Use the white noise generator to create drum and percussive effects. Drums are short and sharp. What attack and decay will you need? Alter the filter so that the sound becomes less 'hissing' and more like a drum. It is up to you to decide how deep you want the drum to sound.
2 Perhaps you could make up your own drum rhythms to accompany other instruments or singing.

Synthesizer or organ?

There is very little that separates some synthesizers from what we should more properly call organs. There are some instruments that are a mixture of the two. These have some sounds that are pre-set and unalterable and other sounds that can be changed by using filters and an envelope.

One of the most popular (and cheapest) mini-keyboards is the Casio VL 1. This was launched in 1981 and was originally designed as a calculator! As well as a miniature keyboard which is monophonic it also has pre-set drum rhythms rather like a home organ. It is not a full synthesizer, as the basic sounds are pre-set, however, it can alter the envelope of some sounds and so create its own sounds. It also has the ability to memorize short tunes that are played on it. A German pop group called Trio used the Casio VL 1 as the main instrument in their hit song 'Da Da Da' in 1981.

▲ Casio VL 1 memorizing keyboard

The Yamaha MK100 is not a full synthesizer but it has many features that you would find on a synthesizer. The basic sounds are set but they can be altered by adding certain pre-set waveforms and envelope shapes. You are able to make up your own drum rhythms and the MK100 will remember tunes and songs that you play or compose yourself.

Some manufacturers used parts of electronic organs combined with synthesizers to create special instruments; e.g. string synthesizers, drum synthesizers, and electronic pianos. However, it must be pointed out that much of the sound of these has been pre-set by the manufacturer in an attempt to imitate real instruments. They are not therefore true synthesizers.

Sequencing

Many synthesizers can remember the notes that you play. If your playing is not very accurate then you can play the notes one by one. As you play each note you tap in the number of beats the note should last, usually on a special button. The synthesizer matches the two together and can play back your tune with, we hope, the correct rhythm. This is called **sequencing**.

What has just been described is sequencing in **step-time** because it is done step by step. Some synthesizers are able to store tunes as you play them which is a much quicker process. This is called **real-time** sequencing. There are several programs that can turn your micro-computer into either a real- or step-time sequencer. Later on in this book you will see that your micro-computer can also play synthesizers in this way.

▼ Yamaha MK100

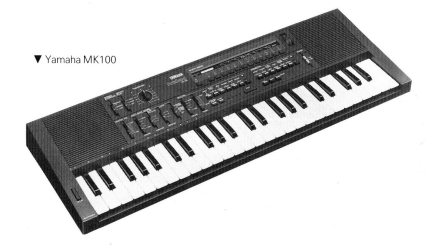

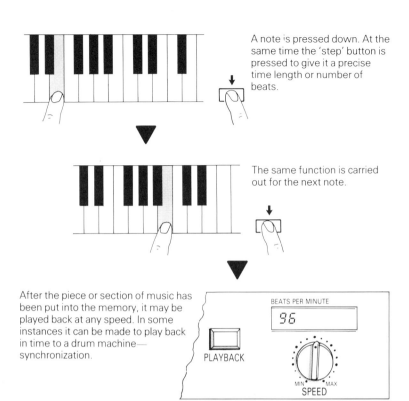

A note is pressed down. At the same time the 'step' button is pressed to give it a precise time length or number of beats.

The same function is carried out for the next note.

After the piece or section of music has been put into the memory, it may be played back at any speed. In some instances it can be made to play back in time to a drum machine—synchronization.

PLAYBACK

BEATS PER MINUTE

96

MIN MAX
SPEED

One of the first hit records to use sequenced music was 'I feel love' by Donna Summer. The drums and repeated musical phrases that were the main part of the record were created entirely by sequenced synthesizers. There is another version of the same song by Mark Almond and Bronski Beat which uses the same method.

The son of the famous French film composer Maurice Jarre, Jean-Michel, has recorded several albums of electronic music, notably *Equinoxe* and *Oxygene*. Both albums use sequenced music. The melodies are played on top of many sequenced patterns. He took his whole show to China and played to astonished audiences there, many of whom had not heard any electronic music before.

▲ Jean-Michel Jarre with a Fairlight (see page 33).

Digital synthesizers and micro-computers

Synthesizers have become cheaper and more sophisticated. Many of the things that a small synthesizer is capable of doing would have taken rooms full of bulky equipment only twenty years ago. At least two new synthesizers now appear every month. Until quite recently most synthesizers used electricity to create and control the sound (voltage control). Electronic music has now entered another exciting period, that of digital synthesis—using computer language to create sound (digital control).

All the synthesizers we have discussed have used electricity as the means of creating the vibrations and waveforms which are the fundamental part of sound. This is called **analog** synthesis. However, since 1960 it has been

▼ Micro-computer linked with Yamaha DX7, Oberheim Xpander and Yamaha RX15 drums.

possible to create sound using large computers. Computers use a special language to transmit data inside themselves. This language is digital, in other words it uses numbers transmitted in special codes at high speed.

By using certain programs it was discovered that the high speed of a computer could digitally create waveforms similar to those created on an analog synthesizer. The main advantage is that the computer can do many things with digital code. It can store the sounds created in its memory. It can show you the waveforms on its screen. It can show you the envelope of the sound. The big computers create a far better quality of synthesized sound and it is easy for digital synthesizers to memorize sounds and sequenced patterns.

The main problem that electronic composers had in the early 1960s was that computers were still large and very expensive. The age of the micro-chip had not yet occurred. That is why the analog type of synthesizer was developed and became available first.

The American composer and performer Gordon Mumma was one of the first people to design the electronic circuitry that enabled a computer to be used by a performer on stage. The music is created by a combination of the performer and the computer-synthesizer. This creates a live, almost instant composition. He calls this **cybersonics**. The music he created like this was fist performed in 1965, and he has continued to work with computers and synthesizers, especially in live performances.

There are many types of digital synthesizers now available. All the manufacturers of synthesizers are making different versions of digital synthesizers. Digital synthesizers are often made to look similar to analog synthesizers so that the performer can feel at home with the instrument.

Yamaha DX synthesizers

Many pop groups and electronic music studios use DX synthesizers because of their unique sound capabilities. Launched in 1983, the Yamaha series of DX synthesizers was the first to use what is called **frequency modulation** (FM for short). Instead of combining different waveforms to create sound as we have seen in analog synthesizers, and some digital synthesizers, the DX series uses only one waveform. It uses a sine wave. By combining several sine waves in different ways it is possible to create very complex waveforms not possible before. It imitates other instruments but does not actually copy by using sound samples. The sound produced is very close to that of the instrument imitated because of the complicated waveforms it is able to produce. It can also have a touch-sensitive keyboard (a keyboard similar to that of a piano). The harder and faster you press the note the louder and more percussive the sound becomes. The possibilities using this system are almost infinite.

▲ Yamaha DX7

▼ Roland Juno 106

The Roland Juno 106 synthesizer, shown on this page, is a programmable polyphonic synthesizer. It uses a digitally controlled oscillator (DCO) to generate the sound. This replaces the voltage controlled oscillator (VCO) on earlier synthesizers. It is very similar to the diagram that we have seen of the basic synthesizer. It uses sliding controls which helps the performer to feel at home with this new type of synthesizer. When the player has created a sound it can be stored in a memory. This instrument can remember 128 different sounds all of which have been created by the performer. It is possible to transfer this memory to a cassette tape recorder. This means that a voice library can be built up on cassettes.

◄ Gordon Mumma performing *Cybersonic Cantilevers* at Everson Museum, Syracuse, New York, 20 May 1973.

Questions

1 What two methods of sequencing are there?
2 Why did the analog synthesizer develop first?
3 What is the main advantage of a digital synthesizer?

The makers of synthesizers could see that they were in danger of making too many synthesizers that went out of date quickly. Digital synthesizers offered them a great possibility to help each other.

With analog synthesizers it had been possible to link them together in some form or other. This had made synchronizing drum machines and sequencers much easier. This was proving to be a bad idea. Sales were falling because people did not know which system to use and they did not wish to be tied to one particular make.

The manufacturers decided to get together and create a common synthesizer language—MIDI.

MIDI is short for **Musical Instrument Digital Interface**. It is a standard that most synthesizer manufacturers agreed on in 1982. It means that you can now connect different synthesizers together to create more complex sounds. It also means that home micro-computers can be connected to synthesizers to control them. There is a rapidly expanding variety of devices available to link up computers and synthesizers. It is also possible to link drum machines up to synthesizers via a MIDI interface so that drums, bass, and chords can be synchronized together. The synthesizers can be controlled using digital codes passed along the connecting cables. In this way up to sixteen synthesizers and a micro-computer can work together. MIDI is being used as an increasingly complex means of communication between instruments.

Micro-computers controlling several synthesizers

The volume and sensitivity of each instrument can be changed by the computer while the piece is being performed. It is even possible to change the complete sound of each instrument by putting the appropriate instruction in the controlling computer.

The composer can use a special program that enables him to write a separate music line for each synthesizer. The program also enables the composer to alter the sound of each synthesizer as the piece is played. The score is displayed on the monitor screen and moves from right to left as the piece is played. The computer can be made to add or take away notes that the composer does not want. There are more and more programs and interfaces becoming available. The important thing when considering such programs is that they must be easy for someone to use. In computer terms they should be user-friendly.

Most of the programs allow the composer to put each note in from the synthesizer keyboard and then tell the micro-computer how long and loud that note should be. This is called programming in **step-time**. Some programs allow each line to be written in **real-time**. The program acts like a tape recorder and records every note played. The program can then compensate for any slight inaccuracies and align the notes so that the synthesizers are synchronized and sound together.

Howard Jones

Originally trained on piano, the singer-songwriter Howard Jones uses many synthesizers and sequencers during his concerts. His first tour in fact was a solo tour. All the instruments and sounds were created by using sequencers, drum machines etc. The keyboards were then played live over the sequenced backing. He allowed some flexibility when he programmed the backing so that each performance could be slightly different.

▼ Howard Jones

Tangerine Dream

One of the first groups to use only synthesizers and no other instruments were Tangerine Dream from Germany. They have been playing together since 1967 and have produced many records which explore the use of sound. On stage they use many synthesizers both large and small. Their music is used for the television series *Streethawk*.

Breakdance records and other records like this use purely electronic sounds. They employ many aspects of sound synthesis to create an interesting catalogue of effects over the insistent energetic rhythm track. It is an interesting use of sounds for their own sake. Some of the records use a 'scratch' technique where a record is moved by hand with the needle on it. This adds to the sound picture being created.

Records to listen to: the soundtrack of the film *Beat Street* and Herbie Hancock's *Rockett*.

▼ Tangerine Dream (*left to right*: Michael Hoenig, Edgar Froese, Christoph Franke).

▲ ▼ Break-dancing

Yamaha CX5

This is the first home micro-computer and synthesizer that is all in one, with a piano-type keyboard. It has several programs that create an infinite variety of sounds. It can also replay the music written into it using up to eight different sounds at the same time. It is fitted with a MIDI interface on the back so that it can also control other synthesizers, and has an FM chip. It has a graphic display which can be used to help create more sounds.

▼ Yamaha CX5

Fairlight computer synthesizer

This is one of the most expensive and sophisticated computer synthesizers available. Before it appeared the only computer music systems available were very large and often very complex to use. It has virtually every possible feature contained within it. One of its most impressive features is the ability to listen to a sound and synthesize it digitally. This is called **sound sampling**. For example if you were to bang a piece of metal it would recreate that sound digitally so that it is then possible for the computer to turn it into a sound that can be played on the keyboard.

It is widely used by composers and pop musicians alike. Amongst pop musicians using it are Peter Gabriel, Stevie Wonder, Duran Duran, Culture Club and Frankie goes to Hollywood. There are also synthesizers which can record and replay sounds via a keyboard. They record sound digitally so it can be altered to create totally new sounds. Sometimes the

▼ A diagram of how a computer analyses and samples sounds. It splits the sound up into very tiny portions and then remembers each little portion.

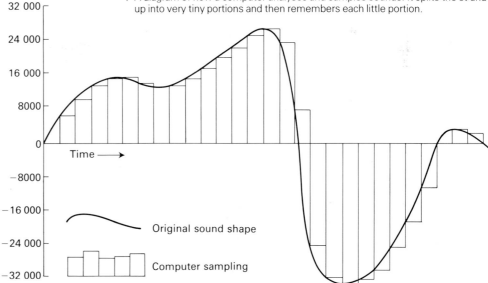

▲ Fairlight founders/inventors: Kim Ryrie (*left*) and Peter Vogel with the Series III CMI.

▲ Vince Clarke (ex-Yazoo) with a Fairlight

sound can be repeated without a break; this is called **looping**.

The Fairlight can do many other things besides sampling; it can be used as a conventional synthesizer, a sequencer and a drum machine all in one. You can also draw the shape of the sound you want on the screen. Sound sampling is now being used to create sound effects in films.

Depeche Mode use mainly synthesizers for their live performances. They use a mixture of synthesized and sampled sound. Quite often the sample-sounds are those that they have used on their records resampled onto their stage synthesizers.

▲ Depeche Mode in 1985

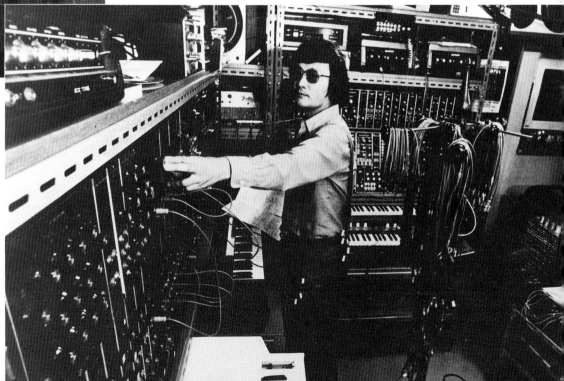

Tomita ▶

Questions

1 What do the letters MIDI stand for?
2 Why is it useful for synthesizers to have a MIDI interface?
3 What is a Fairlight?
4 What is sound sampling?

Projects

1 Listen to some synthesized versions of classical music by either Isao Tomita or Walter Carlos. Compare them with recordings of the same pieces performed by orchestras. Which do you prefer? Why? Do you think that music sounds better on the instruments for which it was written?

Creating music on the micro-computer and using it as a synthesizer

Most people are now familiar with the micro-computer. These are cheap and powerful chips that can do as much if not more than their large predecessors. Along with this development came digital sound chips, chips that created sound. These were first heard in the space invaders type of game. Very quickly they became part of most home computers. At the same time better versions of sound chips were made for digital synthesizers.

The micro-computer has three separate functions in synthesized music:

a It can create sounds with its own sound chip.
b It can be connected via a MIDI interface to a digital synthesizer and control the synthesizer.
c It can sample sound by using an interface.

Most micro-computers have a sound chip or some means of generating sound digitally. Some machines are able to do this better than others depending on the power of the chip inside it. The best micro-computers for sound are either the Commodore 64 or the BBC model B. These micro-computers are able to generate three voices at once as well as having a noise channel for sound effects. Both add envelope shaping to the sound created.

The Commodore has a special chip called SID which has been specially designed for sound generation. It is able to create slightly better waveforms as well as having a filter.

It is as well to remember that the sound of micro-computers is improved by using additional amplifiers and speakers. The Spectrum and the BBC benefit greatly from this. The Commodore sound comes from the TV speakers but even this can be improved. A good tip in this case is to retune the TV set slightly which should improve the sound although usually at the expense of a clear picture.

There are several programs available for most micro-computers which will turn your micro into a simple synthesizer. In some cases it will enable the micro-computer to memorize the tunes you play; it uses the power of the micro-computer as a sequencer. There are also keyboards available for micro-computers. Some of these fit over the standard typewriter keys, others (more expensive) are piano-type keyboards that plug into the micro. Sometimes the keyboard also has some sound-generating chips of its own. It will then borrow the power of the micro to shape and filter the sound.

It is now possible to buy sound sampling devices that fit on to some micro-computers. All the indications are that many of the synthesizer and micro-computer manufacturers will be developing sound sampling devices that will connect between synthesizer and micro-computer. Doubtless there will be more and more programs available. More powerful micro-computers are now available with greater musical capabilities. It seems certain that many micro-computers will have a MIDI interface fitted to them as standard.

▲ Yamaha HS500

▼ Yamaha MPI

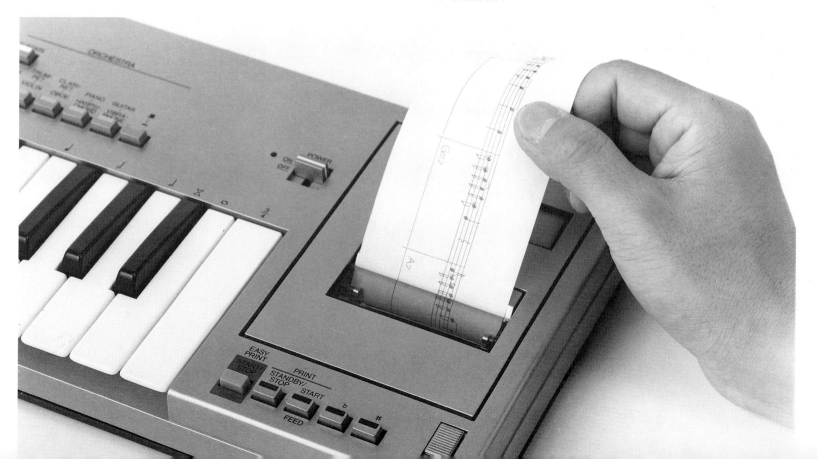

Music notation

Music for conventional instruments like the piano, recorder, or violin is relatively easy to read and write. The system for writing music has been with us for several hundred years and works very well. But how do you write out the sounds that are created by a synthesizer?

Music is written out so that other people can play it. If there is no need for anybody else to perform a piece, for example if the work is recorded on tape, then there is no need for the music to be written down. However, some electronic music uses both synthesizers and other instruments. So there is a need for some kind of written music so that the performance can be co-ordinated. This is often done with a sort of graph that shows blocks of sound. One of the first composers to use this idea was Karlheinz Stockhausen. Stockhausen often includes the details of how each sound was created.

Generally the notation of electronic music is necessary for

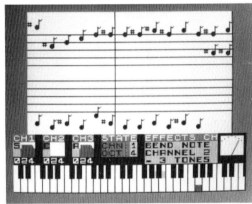

▲ How a computer may present a score on screen.

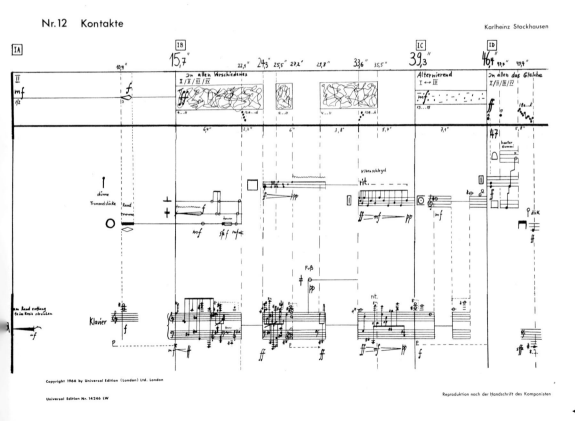

Nr.12   Kontakte

Karlheinz Stockhausen

Copyright 1966 by Universal Edition (London) Ltd. London

Universal Edition Nr. 14246 LW

Reproduktion nach der Handschrift des Komponisten

◄ Stockhausen's score of *Kontakte*

'live' performance. By using a computer as a sequencer to control the synthesizer the problem of writing out electronic music has nowadays largely been avoided. Computers which are attached to synthesizers by an interface device like MIDI can also be used to print conventional music. This is not as good as the presently used methods of writing down music but is an area which is being developed and it will not be long before software is available which will enable us to print music direct from a computer to as high a standard as conventionally printed music.

Synthesizers that teach

The world-famous conductor Leopold Stokowski wrote in 1930 'It is only a few years before we shall have entirely new methods of tone production (making musical sounds) by electrical means . . . Thus will begin a new era in music . . . One wonderful feature of the new electric instruments is, or will be, the practical absence of technical difficulty in playing them. There will be no long hours of practice every day, electricity will do all the mechanical part.'

Synthesizers can be linked to teaching programs. In this way learning how to read and play music can be taught with the aid of computer. Perhaps software will be developed to teach music skills. More advanced programs could teach particular pieces and show the player where mistakes occur. In many ways this will take the drudgery out of learning and make it more fun to learn. It will be possible to link all sorts of instruments to teaching computers, using the technology developed in sound synthesis and computing.

Cinema and film

Many films in recent years have used synthesizers for their music. For example *Close Encounters of the Third Kind* uses a synthesizer to communicate with the Aliens. However, electronics have been used in films for many years. Both the theremin and the ondes martenot were featured in many films after 1945. The recent popularity of science-fiction films has meant that electronics have played an increasingly important role.

Films to look out for:

King Kong (1933) uses theremin. Max Steiner.

The Lost Weekend and *Spellbound* (1945). Both these films use a theremin as part of the score. *Spellbound* won an Academy Award for its music. Miklos Rozsa.

The Day the Earth Stood Still (1951). Four theremins plus an electronic oscillator. Bernard Hermann.

Forbidden Planet (1956). Bebe Barron.

Chariots of Fire (1981). Vangelis.

Tron (1981). Wendy Carlos.

The BBC Radiophonic Workshop is an important part of electronic music making in the United Kingdom. Many programmes that the BBC make use electronic soundtracks. These are nearly always created in the Radiophonic Workshop. One of its best known pieces is the theme tune for the series *Dr Who* which was first heard in 1963.

Projects

1 Write the outline of a short story on one of the following subjects:
   a Lost in space
   b Walking on a hot summer's day
   c In the city at night
2 When you have written the outline imagine that it is to be made into a short film or video. Decide at which points in the story you need music and sound. Using either a synthesizer or micro-computer, make up sounds and short tunes for each part of the story. It may even be possible to act out the story and add the sound and music during the performance.

4 The future

Live performance

Imagine a concert of the future. The stage is dimly lit. Strange sounds surround the audience. As the sound gets louder a shape appears on stage. It is a moving circle of light. As the music gets louder the stage becomes brighter, changing colour. The whirling light seems to hover above the stage and begins to move over the audience. As it hovers in mid-air the sounds change and sometimes sound like human voices. The music now appears to be coming from different parts of the hall at the same time. A spaceship appears on stage and moves with sound towards the hovering white shape. All the time the music is changing. Sounds move from every direction.

All this is possible. No human being is playing the music. It is all sequenced and pre-written into the computers and synthesizers. The lights are linked to the synthesizers and computers and change in response to the sounds created. The only problem is that however wonderful the effects and sounds the performance will lack a feeling that something is really happening. When we go to a pop or classical concert there is always a feeling of excitement, the musicians are performing and we are listening to that live performance. If performances of the future are to be given merely by computer then a large part of the excitement will be lost.

Many synthesizer groups and performers realize this. Live performances of the future will therefore have players using synthesizers as both sequencers for a piece of music and as real-time instruments. Perhaps a performer could play a short section of music. The synthesizer will respond to this by playing back an answer. The piece is being re-composed every time. The performer has to respond to that in the same way that a concert pianist has to respond to an orchestra.

◀ Tangerine Dream

Although he may have played the work many times before each time will be a little different. There will be that live element, the human being using skill and imagination to create music.

Whatever happens in the future of electronic music and synthesizers it seems certain that more facilities for creating music will become available at far cheaper prices. With the beginning of small flat televisions it will not be long before one of these is incorporated into a synthesizer that will show the exact shape of the sound created and will also display the music written. More powerful chips are being developed. These will offer more sound, more power to the composer at a far cheaper level than could have been imagined only a few years ago.

Throughout the development of the synthesizer it has become more and more apparent that the importance of the composer is far greater than the performer. We can use the power of the micro-computer and electronic chip to help us to perform the music. It can help us remember the sounds we have made and even correct minor mistakes made. How long will it be before the computer takes over and writes its own music?

The computer can be fed information on how certain types of music are written. Given a formula for doing this very powerful computers can produce tunes and even a whole piece. What a computer cannot do is imagine. It has been said that writing music is 5% inspiration and 95% perspiration! Synthesizers offer us more sounds than we can imagine and give us more for our imagination to work on. Computers can help us remove some of the hard work from writing out and remembering the music, but they are incapable of being inspired. They are extensions of human imagination and skill. The most important part of any piece of music is the imagination and skill of the composer in creating a work.

Video synthesizers

The idea of linking colour and music is not new. For centuries many attempts have been made to link music to colour and pictures. There have been many types of colour organs that flashed coloured lights and shapes when certain keys and notes are played.

The most obvious example of this is the flashing lights in discotheques. These are very often linked to particular pitches in the music, often the drums. In this way the lights appear to flash in time to the music. It is possible that computers linked directly to synthesizers can be made to create graphic displays, shapes and effects in response to the music being played.

Even as you read this there are new synthesizers being developed. Some of them will be very expensive and it is unlikely that we will be lucky enough to play them ourselves. What is important is that the big expensive synthesizers lead to the synthesizers which we can play at home and school. Some composers think that ultimately there will be just one type of synthesizer. There will be different makes but they will all have the same sorts of features. It is in your lifetime that many of the major compositions for the synthesizer will take place. Who knows, it could be you that creates some of them.

Projects

Here are three further projects for you to try. These may be tackled in a variety of ways.

They can be created on one synthesizer using a multi-tracking recorder—whereby one part is recorded, the second added on top of it, and so on, building up to the whole piece. If you have not used such a piece of equipment before, get someone who has to help you. It can be very frustrating to find that your efforts are distorted or inaudible.

It is possible to perform the projects on four synthesizers in a live situation using one synthesizer to create the noises. Depending on the synthesizers used it may be possible to change sounds in performance if the synthesizers have programmable memories.

If you are fortunate enough to own some MIDI-compatible synthesizers it is possible to enter the music into a computer and, via a suitable interface and software, you can drive the synthesizer (or synthesizers) from the computer, perhaps leaving one part to be played live. The exact method of entering the music will depend on the particular interface and computer used.

If your computer can generate three channels of sound plus one of noise (e.g. BBC, Commodore, Amstrad) you can either enter the notes directly or use one of the special music programs that are commercially available which would be a lot easier and save a lot of time.

With these projects it is possible to add real drums and percussion, to use a drum machine or to create your own percussive sounds on the synthesizer or computer. If you do, use a suitable rhythm pattern that fits with the sound and atmosphere needed. You may like to take some of these suggestions a little further and devise your own pieces. Remember that there are many ways a composer who works with electronics approaches composing a piece, just as a composer who works with acoustic and orchestral instruments does. Along with an appealing melody or rhythm is an overall structure or form which the piece will take. It is always best to note down the way in which your favourite sounds were created. When using a computer or certain types of synthesizer it is possible to store the sounds on data cassette or disk. If so make a backup copy.

Grimcastle

The following is a brief description of a new computer game. You have been asked to create the sounds required for the game, the parts of which are listed below. Invent your own graphic score for each sound.

Cybernaught must overcome the evil Timelord of Grimcastle and rescue the mystical fifth dimension synthesizer, located in the Timelord's great hall. To do this he must enter the castle avoiding burning oil, and laser spears. Entrance to the castle is either over the drawbridge or through the secret door—only opened with the magic password. Once inside the castle, sinister music plays constantly and Cybernaught must avoid the robotic crossbow and the Timelord himself, who fights with bolts of lightning.

Sounds required:

1 Short, simple tune or noise for the game's title screen (5 seconds).
2 A repetitive sound every time Cybernaught moves.
3 Burning oil (2 seconds).
4 Laser spears (0.5 seconds + explosion).
5 Cybernaught hit and killed—a slow thin wailing sound (4 seconds), followed by gloomy vibrating sound accompanying screen display of 'Cybernaught has failed'.
6 Drawbridge up and down—a sound like chains creaking (1 second).
7 Secret door opens—magical mystic sound (2 seconds).
8 Sinister castle music—sound/noise repeated and continuously looped.
9 Crossbow firing arrows—half a second and noise of target being hit (1 second).
10 Timelord—low noise and thunder (1 second).
11 Synthesizer rescued—fanfare (3 seconds).

The Presto advertisement

The Lashup motor car company are launching a new car, the Presto. The television advertisement will use electronic music. A brief description of the advert follows with the music cues required. You are asked to provide the music.

The advertisement shows the car starting in the early morning summer mist. After a glimpse of the sunrise the car drives through the countryside. The impression is fast and powerful, the car is on a rough but wide road. The car then makes an emergency stop as a ferry bridge is unexpectedly raised in front of it. The journey proceeds smoothly and calmly, driving onto a beach for a peaceful and tranquil sunset, sailing ships are seen in the background. A voice announces the Presto followed by a short tune that can be identified as the Presto Tune and will be used in future promotions.

Cues:

1 Misty, slow sound.
2 Sunrise—single note building up to a big warm sound.
3 Driving—steady pulsating rhythm with occasional sharp percussive sounds.
4 Surprise percussive sound for emergency stop.
5 Smoother but still pulsating rhythm for rest of journey, getting calmer and building to a big sound for car appearing on the beach. This fades to a single high smooth note for the sunset, almost imitating the beginning.
6 Presto tune—about 5 seconds long.

Another Serial

D.S. al Fine

The accompanying music score for *Another Serial* is written out for you to perform on whatever equipment you have available.

The noise part has been written out in graphic form illustrating the sounds required with ideas for the sounds and noises at the end of the piece. These are to be taken as suggestions—you may interpret them as you want. Some other ideas that you could try with this piece are:

a Try each part with a different sound from the one indicated—afterwards you could swap the sounds for the parts around. Make a note of the combination that sounds the best.

b Try changing fast attacking sounds for ones with slow attacks. What happens? Does it change the piece?

c You could alter the noise part completely and invent your own. It is possible to change the sounds as you perform the piece.

Suggested sounds

Channel 1—Bright strings or brass.
Channel 2—Piano type sound that will sustain without decay.
Channel 3—Synthesizer bass sound with hard attack.

Noise: interpretation of symbols

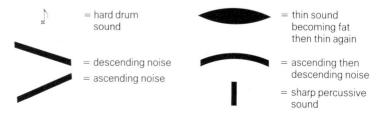

= hard drum sound

= thin sound becoming fat then thin again

= descending noise
= ascending noise

= ascending then descending noise

= sharp percussive sound

Important dates and events in the history of the synthesizer

1906   Thaddeus Cahill invents the dynamophone.

1920   Leon Theremin invents and demonstrates the theremin in Petrograd (now Leningrad), USSR

1924   The first work for the theremin is performed.

1928   The ondes martenot is developed and demonstrated.

1934   *Ecuatorial* is composed by Varèse.

1948   Messiaen composes *Turangalîla-symphonie* which uses an ondes-martenot.

1950   The first tape recorder is commercially available.

1951   The world's first electronic music studio is set up in Cologne.

1952   The RCA synthesizer is built in America.

1954   Stockhausen writes *Studie* for electronically created sounds.

1961   The first computer program is written that enables sound to be created digitally. It was developed by the Bell Telephone Company in America.

1963   The transistor is now cheap enough to be used in everyday goods.

1963   Robert Moog develops the idea of voltage control and modular synthesis.

1965   Gordon Mumma uses cybersonics to enable music to be played and controlled by computer.

1968   *Switched on Bach* is recorded by Walter Carlos. It uses only synthesizers and is a best selling record.

1970   The Mini-Moog becomes available.

1970   Emerson Lake and Palmer tour and record using Moog synthesizers.

1974   First polyphonic synthesizer is launched.

1977   First programmable synthesizer is available.

1979   Fairlight Computer Synthesizer is made available.

1980   The start of micro-computers for the home.

1982   MIDI agreed as an international synthesizer and computer interface standard.

1983   Digital synthesizers become widely and cheaply available.

1985   Cheaper sound-sampling synthesizers become available. Much hardware is launched that can make home micro-computers capable of sophisticated sound synthesis, sound sampling, sequencing, composing and printing.

1986   Atari ST computer is produced with a built-in MIDI. MIDI software is available to a much wider market, including home computers.

1988   Synthesizers can be used in general music examinations in Great Britain.

Glossary of terms used in the book

ADSR: attack–decay–sustain–release—the most common form of envelope shaper.

Amplitude: the size of a sound signal, usually the same as volume.

Analog: continuously variable, a synthesizer that uses electricity (voltage) as a means of creating and controlling the sound. The other way of creating sound is digitally (using computer language).

Attack: the first stage of an envelope—the time it takes for the envelope to rise from its initial level to its maximum level.

Auto correct: a facility found on sequencers that enables the timing of the notes to be corrected to the nearest part of a beat. It prevents inaccuracies that could occur in real-time sequencing (also called **Quantize**).

Basic: the programming language that is most frequently used in micro-computers.

Bending: raising or lowering the pitch of a note. Usually only meant when the note is bent a small amount.

Cartridge memory: a plug-in electronic memory pack that is used instead of a cassette memory.

Cassette memory: a device that enables digital information to be stored onto an ordinary audio cassette. It is often used to store voice libraries or sequences. It is very similar to the way in which micro-computers can store programs on cassette.

Clock: a device that sends a pulse to several synthesizers (or from one instrument to another). It will ensure that all the instruments will play in perfect synchronization. It is often a micro-computer that acts as a clock.

Controller: something that gives you musical control over the synthesizer. In most cases this is a keyboard. In some cases it could be a computer.

Control voltage: the electricity that is used to control the various parts of a synthesizer. For example the voltage controlled amplifier (VCA) receives certain amounts of electricity at certain times according to how the envelope is set up.

Cut-off frequency: the frequency around which a filter will operate.

DC: digitally controlled, the sound is created or modified by using computer language.

Decay: the second stage of the sound envelope, the time which the sound takes to fall back from its maximum level to the sustain level.

Envelope: the shape of the final sound. (See **ADSR**)

Frequency modulation: a method of synthesizing sound by combining several similar waveforms.

Filter: a device that adjusts the tone of the basic sound produced by the oscillator. It works by blocking out the unwanted frequencies.

Glissando: an automatic effect, causing the pitch of the note to slide between two consecutive notes.

Harmonics: the frequencies above the basic note which also sound when the note is played. All instruments have them. On synthesizers they have to be added to the basic sound by using filters and extra oscillators. Also called **Overtones**.

Keyboard split: two sounds can be played simultaneously at each side of a pre-determined split point.

LFO: low frequency oscillator, often used in conjunction with the VCO or VCF to create either vibrato or tremolo effects (see also **Modulation**).

MIDI: Musical Instrument Digital Interface. An international standard which allows information to be passed between synthesizers and computers of different makes.

Modifier: any part of the synthesizer that changes the basic sound created by the oscillator.

Modulation: adding another frequency or waveform to a sound already created by the oscillator. It has the effect of modifying the sound.

Monophonic: capable of only playing one note at a time.

Oscillator: the vibrating unit of the synthesizer which gives the basic sound—usually with a choice of waveforms.

Overtones: see **Harmonics**.

Patch: the particular setting required by a synthesizer to create a specific sound.

Pitch: the highness or lowness of a note, measured in feet and derived from the length of an organ pipe that would produce that sound; sometimes referred to by note name and octave number.

Pitch bend: see **Bending**.

Pitch control: the overall tuning adjustment.

Polyphonic: capable of playing more than two notes at the same time.

Programmable: a programmable synthesizer is one that can memorize the settings of its controls so that particular sounds created can be quickly recalled by one or two actions.

Quantize: see **Auto correct**.

Release: the fourth stage of the envelope generator. It allows the sound to carry on after the note has been released.

Resonance: part of the filter section; it boosts certain frequencies to change the tone of the sound.

Sampling: recording a short section of sound digitally. It can then be manipulated by a computer or certain types of synthesizer to recreate or modify the sound sampled at any pitch.

Sawtooth: type of waveform with this shape:

Sequencer: a device which can memorize all the information a synthesizer needs to play back a previously composed pattern of notes.

Sine: type of waveform with this shape:

Sound source: see **Oscillator**.

Square: type of waveform with this shape:

Sustain: the third stage of the envelope generator. It defines how long the note will remain whilst the key is played.

Tremolo: an effect in which the filtering is slightly pulsed by a LFO causing the sound to fade rapidly and return.

VC: Voltage control. A synthesizer that uses voltage to control the means of creating or altering the sound.

VCF: voltage controlled filter.

VCA: voltage controlled amplifier.

VCO: voltage controlled oscillator.

Vibrato: an effect in which the pitch of the note played is raised and lowered slightly giving a wobbly effect. The speed is usually controlled by the LFO.

Waveform: types of oscillations produced by the VCO; each waveform having a different basic sound and shape.

White noise: a hissing sound rather like a radio tuned off station. It is actually created by fast random selections of all frequencies, sounds and waveforms that we can hear.

Further reading

Magazines

Music Technology (formerly *Electronics and Music Maker*) Published monthly by Music Maker Publications.
Sound on Sound Published by SOS Publications Ltd.

Books

There are many books now available on the subject and this is by no means a comprehensive list. However it may prove to be a starting point.

The Complete Synthesizer Handbook by Michael Norman and Ben Dickey, published by Zomba Books.
The Synthesizer and Electronic Keyboard Handbook by David Crombie, published by Dorling Kindersley.
The Musician and The Micro by Ray Hammond, published by Blandford Press.
The BBC Radiophonic Workshop by Desmond Briscoe and Roy Curtis-Bramwell, published by BBC Publications.
Will You Still Love Me When I'm 64? (A book about making music on the Commodore 64) by Peter Gerrard, Published by Duck Press.
Micro-computers in Music Education by Nick Pickett, obtainable from Capital Region Information Centre, John Ruskin Street, London, SE5 0PQ.
Making Music on the BBC Micro by Ian Waugh, published by Sunshine Books.
Keyboard Synthesizer Library by the Editors of *Keyboard Magazine*, published by Hal Leonard.

In addition to these there are many books available on how to play simple melodies and tunes on synthesizers. The majority of these do not take into account the way in which sound is synthesized or created. They are usually adaptations from single keyboard or organ teach-yourself books.

Most synthesizer manufacturers have handbooks and explanations of sound synthesis. These are often written with a particular synthesizer in mind. However, they will be only too pleased to be of assistance with your enquiries.